# Enneagram for Beginners

A Self-Discovery Guide for Personal Growth and Spiritual Development

# Table of Contents

# Peface

xplore the wonderful world of the Enneagram and unlock the secrets of your true self.

Have you always been awed by the wisdom of the Enneagram?

Are you ready to discover that there's much more to yourself than you're consciously aware of?

Have you always wished there could be some efficient way to experience personal and spiritual growth?

This book will act as a torch, shining a bright light on the complex, intricate maze that is your human psyche. It will give you all the tools you need to embark on a successful, productive journey of self-discovery and self-mastery.

# Introduction

The Enneagram is a powerful tool for self-mastery that has helped so many people like you. The book you hold in your hand will share the transformative wisdom encoded in the Enneagram with you and make you aware of strengths you never knew you had. One thing is certain: By putting the information in this book to work, your life will never remain the same. It will change for the better, and the evolution you experience will be a never-ending one.

Unlike other books on the Enneagram, this one is deliberately written in a way that's easy to understand. Whether you've just learned about this tool or want to study it more, this guide has treasures to explore and enjoy. The guidance in these pages is clear. At no point will you feel confused about what you're learning or what you need to do to take advantage of the knowledge herein.

Your life is about to make a lot more sense. These pages will hand you the cheat codes to a life worth living, showing you what you need to do to handle both the good times and the bad with as much grace and ease as possible. You'll finally stop swimming against the current of life and learn the rewards of going with your personal flow.

Are you prepared to learn the truth about yourself? Does the thought of discovering things you never knew about the person in the mirror excite you? Are you prepared to fully embody the person you've always fantasized about being? If your answer to these questions is yes, head on to the first chapter, where your journey begins.

# Chapter 1:

## Introduction to the Enneagram

Have you ever wondered why you have certain tendencies? Are you baffled by the fact that try as you might to change yourself, some things stay the same? What gives? You do everything all the books and personal development "gurus" say you should. Yet, for some reason, you can't quite hack it. You wonder why you can't shake these behaviors despite all the intention and positive thinking in the world.

What if it's not about forcing yourself to conform to society's definition of "right" or "perfect?" What if what you need is to understand what makes you tick? What are your strengths? What about your weaknesses? Can you accept there's no such thing as the perfect person? That's not a bad thing, you know. Everyone has their good and bad sides. That's what makes you human. The Enneagram is a powerful tool to help you heal and grow. It is a mirror, showing you who you are, warts and all. You can use the information it gives you to make meaningful progress toward becoming your ideal self.

## What Is the Enneagram?

"Enneagram" is such a curious-sounding word, isn't it? It comes from the Greek words *ennea*, which means "nine," and *gramma*, meaning "something drawn or written down." Think of it as a treasure map, except the treasure it leads you to isn't gold or diamonds. It's worth more than that. The treasure the Enneagram offers you is an understanding of yourself and the people around you far beyond what you may have ever considered possible.

This ancient tool has been used to classify personalities successfully and show people how to discover what is holding them back from being the best version of themselves. Now, don't expect your life to magically change once you've used it. This process is one that lasts your whole life. Using the Enneagram with the right perspective will be a rewarding endeavor.

Some assume the Enneagram is one more way to restrict you, telling you what to do and what not to do, like a religion. However, that couldn't be further from the truth. If you're concerned this tool is just another way to put you in a box, fret not. The core principles of the Nine-Point Personality System allow for the fact that people are a little too complex to be banished into specific boxes their whole lives. It is built differently from other personality tools, as it will help you break out of the box you've placed yourself into.

## The History of the Enneagram

You can thank Oscar Ichazo for the Enneagram. It occurred to this native of Bolivia and Peru that there had to be more to life than meets the eye. Oscar became fascinated with a certain school of thought regarding philosophy and inner work. His fascination became powerful enough that it moved him to uproot his life and head to Argentina, where he could attend school in Buenos Aires.

After that, he traveled to Asia, collecting bits and pieces of information. Finally, he headed back home to South America. Throughout his travels, he had been picking pieces of the puzzle that would soon be known as the Enneagram, a gift that would offer one and all the secrets to living authentically and being fulfilled.

Oscar spent years putting his ideas together, and when he thought they were concrete enough, he set up the Arica School. Many would come to his school to learn about what he'd discovered. He taught in his school in the late '60s and early '70s. Eventually, Oscar decided it was time to head to the United States, his last residence, as he remained there until he passed away in 2020.

For Ichazo, the Enneagram was a great way to learn how your personality connects to your true essence. It's a way to learn what makes your soul tick and how you may have taken on certain beliefs and habits that cause you to keep your soul from shining bright. His work was also rooted in Western mysticism and philosophy, as he worked with the idea of there being nine divine forms, which are whole and indivisible. These divine forms are usually lost when you become too attached to your beliefs about who you are, what you can or can't do, what you think about others, etc. In other words, they can become distorted when you live life from the ego instead of your divine self. The concept of nine divine forms itself would be distorted as it made its way from ancient Greece to Egypt, morphing into the seven deadly sins. As for why there aren't nine deadly sins, that's one question that has left everyone stumped.

# The Core Principles of the Enneagram

There are principles that guide the Enneagram, which sets this tool apart from others used to classify people's personalities. If you want to use this assessment tool correctly to get the best results, take time to understand its principles.

**Principle 1: There Are Nine Distinct Archetypes.** They show you how you interact with the world and what your outlook on life is. These types are what drive people to make the choices they do.

**Principle 2: There Are Three Centers of Intelligence.** The nine archetypes are classed into these different centers, also called processing centers:

- The instinctive center is also called the gut center. This center is what drives your actions. It's where your basic instinct comes from. Anger is the emotion that drives this center, and types 8, 9, and 1 fall under it.

- The feeling center, or the heart center, is about your self-identity. It also concerns your relationships with others and, of course, all feelings. The emotion driving this center is shame. The types belonging to this center are 2, 3, and 4.

- The thinking center is the head center concerned with making plans, thinking things through, and establishing safety and security. Types 5, 6, and 7 are under the head center, and fear is the emotion that powers it.

**Principle 3: All Nine Types Have a Core Motivation.** These motivations are defined by one's deepest desires and deepest fears. If you're hungry, you look for food. If you're afraid, you seek safety. By understanding the core motivations of each type, you'll know why everyone acts as they do.

**Principle 4: Your Enneagram Type Comes with Wings.** Remember, it makes no sense to say there are exactly nine kinds of people in the world. There's your Enneagram type, and then there are two other types adjacent to yours. You may lean more toward one of them, which would influence how your primary type expresses itself. The other type is called your wing. For instance, you may be a Type 4, leaning toward either 3 or 5. If you lean toward 5, that would make you a 4 with a 5 wing or a "4w5."

**Principle 5: There Are Paths of Integration and Disintegration.** These paths account for the behaviors you display now and then that are unlike you. When you're feeling stressed, you may act in a different way than you would if you were fine. If you're a Type 4 and everything is fine in your life, you may exhibit Type 1 traits, which would be a path of integration. However, when you're struggling, you may display Type 2 traits. In other words, you're on the path of disintegration, where you're exhibiting adverse traits of a different archetype.

**Principle 6: There Are Levels of Development in Each of the Nine Types.** The levels go from the healthiest to the most dysfunctional. Its flexibility makes the Enneagram much better than other systems that label you. It's possible to go up and down these levels, so don't feel like you're doomed. Where you are on the spectrum depends on what you're dealing with in life, how much you've grown, etc.

**Principle 7: There Are Triads in the Enneagram.** Other than the centers of intelligence, you have the Hornevian triads, which show you how each type acts to get things done, and the Harmonic triads, which demonstrate how each type handles conflict.

**Principle 8: Not All Types Act the Same Way.** This system takes into account the fact that other influences, such as wings, culture, childhood, and personal experiences, can cause people of the same type to act differently from one another.

**Principle 9: The Enneagram Is Meant to Help You Evolve into Your Best Self.** It's for the purpose of self-actualizing, not slapping a label on your head. When you know your type, you'll know the challenges to expect and the strengths you have. Armed with this information, you will know what to do to blossom into the best version of you.

**Principle 10: All Types Are Connected.** Sure, each type is different from others, but they're related to one another. There's a flow of energy from one type to the others, and that's why this system is an excellent one, showing the complexity of humanity.

## Why the Enneagram?

Why should you bother using this tool? If you'd like to transform your life by discovering your true self and experiencing personal growth, the Enneagram is a great path to take. For one thing, it will help you learn why you do what you do, what your tendencies are, and what scares you. For another, you'll have an equally clear grasp of others, being able to see things through their eyes and learn what drives them. This knowledge of self and others will do wonders for your relationships, making them more harmonious and fulfilling.

Everyone wants to grow. Everyone wants to be better. The trouble is no one knows how to have consistent personal growth. With the Enneagram, you have a clear map to follow on your way to your actualized self. This map shows you the strengths you can leverage along your path. It warns you of the potential pitfalls you may face so you can prepare for and handle them with grace when the time comes. You'll learn about your paths of integration and disintegration so you know when you're veering off the track and need to make adjustments.

Finally, the Enneagram offers you the one thing that catapults the rest of your life to levels you only dream of right now. It supports your spiritual growth. Everything in life can be traced to a spiritual origin. If you want to experience transformative change on every level, there's no better way than to feed your spiritual self. The Enneagram will show you what you need to do to get in touch with that aspect of yourself. It can lead you to connect with the divine in a way few other things in life can. If you're convinced about working with this system, it's time to learn which type you are.

# Chapter 2:

---

# Discovering Your Enneagram Type

---

## Overview of the Nine Personality Types

This chapter will help you discover your true Enneagram type or archetype. As previously mentioned, there are nine of them. Here's a detailed look at each one.

## Type 1: The Reformer

This person has a strong sense of ethics and justice. They know things can be better and are quick to take action. You can tell you're dealing with a Type 1 from their high standards and how organized they are. These are great attributes, but when a Type 1 is in overdrive, they give in to their critical and perfectionist tendencies. If you're a Type 1, you're a rational person, in control of yourself, and true to your principles.

- **Basic Fear:** Being evil or not good enough
- **Basic Desire:** Acting with integrity, maintaining balance, being a good person

- **Enneagram 1 with a 9-wing:** Idealist
- **Enneagram 1 with a 2-wing:** Advocate
- **Core motivations:** To make everything better, be beyond criticism, and be right

## Type 2: The Helper

The helper cares. No one is more generous than they are. If you're a Type 2, you're warmhearted, and everyone knows it. Your words and actions are rooted in sincerity. Your ability to empathize with others is unparalleled. The trouble is, if you don't watch it, you can become too attached to sentiments. You may find yourself flattering others and acting to please others even if you'd rather not. Generally, you mean well. You want nothing more than to establish deep connections with others, but beware of your tendency to do things for others because you like it when they need you. Moreover, you may be possessive at times and have trouble accepting you have needs you should attend to. Your love for others is true and unconditional when you're at your best.

- **Basic Fear:** Not being wanted or being unworthy of love
- **Basic Desire:** Feeling loved
- **Enneagram 2 with a 1-wing:** Servant

- **Enneagram 2 with a 3-wing:** Host
- **Core motivations:** To be loved, appreciated, needed, and express what they feel for others

## Type 3: The Achiever

Type 3 people are charming. You can tell from how they carry themselves that they're confident in what they do, and this makes them attractive. If you're a Type 3, you're competent, and your ambition matches your abilities. You're bursting with energy. You may also be someone who is keenly aware of your status in life, ever seeking to attain higher levels of achievement. You're quite the diplomat, saying the right things and keeping your composure. Sometimes, you're a little too concerned about the image you present and how others view you. You're probably a workaholic at your worst and may give in to competition no matter the cost.

- **Basic Fear:** Having no worth
- **Basic Desire:** Feeling worthy and treasured
- **Enneagram 3 with a 2-wing:** Charmer
- **Enneagram 3 with a 4-wing:** Professional
- **Core motivations:** Being a cut above others, praised, and noticed

# Type 4: The Individualist

A Type 4 is self-aware. You're also more sensitive than others, but it'd be hard for most people to tell because you're reserved. When it comes to your emotions, you keep things real. Your creativity is unparalleled, and you're excellent with personal connections. So, what's the catch to being a 4? You can be too self-conscious at your worst, which holds you back. You also are rather moody. If you get it in your head that there's something wrong with you or you're not safe, you pull back from others. You may also be self-indulgent and sometimes throw yourself quite the pity party as you wallow in the blues. When you feel your best, nothing can stop you from receiving inspiration and creatively expressing yourself.

- **Basic Fear:** Having no importance of certainty of who they are
- **Basic Desire:** Finding their true selves and learning why they matter
- **Enneagram 4 with a 3-wing:** Aristocrat
- **Enneagram 4 with a 5-wing:** Bohemian
- **Core motivations:** To be an individual, express themselves, handle their emotions first, and have beauty around them

## Type 5: The Investigator

The Type 5 person has their eyes wide open and never misses a trick. If you know someone curious about life and has deep insights, they're probably a 5. They can keep their attention on whatever complex skills they're learning for long, as their ability to concentrate is impressive. If you're a 5, you're an independent person. You have the most creative solutions to problems, and you're lost in your mind creating things, more often than not. People might describe you as being detached sometimes. Other times, you're intense. You struggle with your eccentric side. Sometimes, you feel life is pointless, and you'd rather be by yourself. Type 5 people are visionaries, blazing trails for others to follow.

- **Basic Fear:** Feeling incapable, stuck in a helpless situation, or being of no use
- **Basic Desire:** To demonstrate competence and capability
- **Enneagram 5 with a 4-wing:** Iconoclast
- **Enneagram 5 with a 6-wing:** Problem Solver
- **Core motivations:** To know and understand all things so they can be safe from the world at all times

# Type 6: The Loyalist

The Type-6 person is dependable. When they commit to something, they're unconditionally in it for the long haul. As a Type 6 person, you're a worker bee, and everyone knows they can trust you. If there's trouble brewing, you knew about it eons before anyone else. If anyone needs help getting people to work together, you're the perfect person for the job. However, you have a dark side. You're anxious and can get defensive sometimes. You thrive on stress, and yet, you complain about it. You may have a hard time making decisions from being overly cautious. When you're at your worst, you're a rebel with only one cause: defying whatever or whoever you sense is asserting their will on you. You struggle with believing in yourself and have a hard time believing others. When you're at your best, you have great inner strength you can rely on, and you stand up for yourself and others.

- **Basic Fear:** Being left to their own devices with no one to guide or support them
- **Basic Desire:** To be supported and feel secure
- **Enneagram 6 with a 5-wing:** Defender
- **Enneagram 6 with a 7-wing:** Buddy

- **Core motivations:** To have others' support, feel a sense of security, and defeat anxiety

## Type 7: The Enthusiast

Are you a Type 7? If yes, you're an extrovert. You look on the bright side of life. You fly by the seat of your pants, choosing to go with the flow. People love your optimistic spirit and the fact that you're practical. However, you tend to spread yourself too thin and struggle with being disciplined. You want something new and exciting. As soon as something becomes routine, you check out mentally. You're always on the go. This trait drains you and scatters your focus. When you're doing great, you focus on your many talents, applying them to achieve specific goals. You're satisfied and thankful for where you are.

- **Basic Fear:** Dealing with pain and deprivation
- **Basic Desire:** Being content in a state where they have no more needs
- **Enneagram 7 with a 6-wing:** Entertainer
- **Enneagram 7 with an 8-wing:** Realist
- **Core motivations:** Staying happy, free, excited, and busy, avoiding and getting rid of pain, being part of noteworthy experiences that make their hearts sing

# Type 8: The Challenger

Type 8s are assertive people. You can feel the strength in their aura, and there's no mistaking their confidence in themselves. These are the people who will give you the facts with no frills. If you need someone resourceful, turn to an 8. These protective people have no trouble making decisions to get the ball rolling. The thing about 8s is they tend to lord it over everyone else. When an 8 isn't gracious, they can be egocentric, feeling the need to make everything and everyone around them conform to their will. Sometimes, this desire to control others can lead to confrontations, and an 8s opponent would need steel for a spine because these people can be intimidating. The 8 type may also have a temper problem. They don't like it when they're put in a vulnerable position. When all is fine in their world, they use their strength to others' advantage.

- **Basic Fear:** Being under someone else's control or getting hurt
- **Basic Desire:** Staying safe by having full control of their life
- **Enneagram 8 with a 7-wing:** Maverick
- **Enneagram 8 with a 9-wing:** Bear

- **Core motivations:** To depend on no one but themselves, never give in to weakness and vulnerability, to be in charge of the world around them, and to be number one

## Type 9: The Peacemaker

Type 9 is a go-with-the-flow type of person. They don't have trouble trusting others, and they're usually the ones with cool heads in a room full of chaos. These creative people see the best in every situation and are willing to offer support when you need it. They love peace, which is great until they go too far with the peacekeeping by going along with whatever someone else imposes on them, even when it's not the best course of action. The 9 loves it when things go without a hitch. If there's conflict, expect them to beat a quick path out of it. This peace-loving type can run into problems because of their tendency to minimize issues and remain complacent in the face of adversity. Sometimes, they're the epitome of inertia. Trying to get them to do something is pointless because their stubbornness is unparalleled. When they're at their best, they are great at resolving conflicts and establishing unlikely connections between people.

- **Basic Fear:** Being isolated from everyone else and feeling lost
- **Basic Desire:** Uninterrupted inner peace
- **Enneagram 9 with an 8-wing:** Referee
- **Enneagram 9 with a 1-wing:** Dreamer
- **Core motivations:** To have a harmonious life, stay away from tense situations, keep things the same, and avoid being perturbed

## What's Your Type?

The following is a questionnaire to gauge what your archetype is. The scale for each statement goes from 1 to 5, with 1 being "this isn't me" and 5 being "this is me."

## Type 1

1. Everything is either black or white, right or wrong. There are no shades of gray. [1] [2] [3] [4] [5]
2. Most people think I'm a mature and responsible person. [1] [2] [3] [4] [5]
3. I can't stand it when people disregard the rules or things aren't in order. [1] [2] [3] [4] [5]
4. I must remain ethical and just in all my ways. [1] [2] [3] [4] [5]

## Type 2

1. I feel fulfilled when people need me, and I help them. [1] [2] [3] [4] [5]
2. I've always been able to tell what people feel or what they might need. [1] [2] [3] [4] [5]
3. I've always put others ahead of me, catering to their needs first. [1] [2] [3] [4] [5]
4. The people in my life think I'm a caring, warm person. [1] [2] [3] [4] [5]

## Type 3

1. Nothing matters to me more than being successful and admired for it. [1] [2] [3] [4] [5]
2. I'm aware of my image and want to be seen in a certain light. [1] [2] [3] [4] [5]
3. I have no trouble adapting, and in all I do, I'm efficient. [1] [2] [3] [4] [5]
4. When I set goals and targets, I'm driven to perform excellently. [1] [2] [3] [4] [5]

## Type 4

1. My inner world is a rich one, and I feel things deeply. [1] [2] [3] [4] [5]
2. I get the sense I'm not like others, and no one will ever get me. [1] [2] [3] [4] [5]

3. Expressing myself, being creative, and having beautiful aesthetics around me matter a lot. [1] [2] [3] [4] [5]

4. Sometimes, I overthink about what may be missing from life. [1] [2] [3] [4] [5]

## Type 5

1. I would rather take time to analyze a situation and observe things before I get involved. [1] [2] [3] [4] [5]

2. I am protective of my space and energy. I need a lot of time to myself to recharge. [1] [2] [3] [4] [5]

3. I love learning and understanding everything I can. [1] [2] [3] [4] [5]

4. People think of me as someone with meaningful insights. [1] [2] [3] [4] [5]

## Type 6

1. I always think about the worst thing that could happen. [1] [2] [3] [4] [5]

2. Nothing matters to me in relationships more than trust and loyalty. [1] [2] [3] [4] [5]

3. I can tell when trouble is brewing, and I'm always prepared. [1] [2] [3] [4] [5]

4. I want nothing more than a stable, secure life. [1] [2] [3] [4] [5]

## Type 7

1. People know I'm the one person who can always see the silver lining. [1] [2] [3] [4] [5]
2. I cram my schedule with exciting, fun activities. [1] [2] [3] [4] [5]
3. I hate the thought of missing out or not getting something others have. [1] [2] [3] [4] [5]
4. People say I'm spontaneous and always down for an adventure. [1] [2] [3] [4] [5]

## Type 8

1. I feel better when I'm in control of every situation. [1] [2] [3] [4] [5]
2. If I see injustice, I stand up against it, no questions asked. [1] [2] [3] [4] [5]
3. People think I'm intense and to the point. [1] [2] [3] [4] [5]
4. I love a good challenge. Challenges don't make me back down. They excite me. [1] [2] [3] [4] [5]

## Type 9

1. I would much rather not deal with conflicts. I do all I can to avoid them. [1] [2] [3] [4] [5]

2. I have no problem seeing multiple perspectives, even when they oppose one another. [1] [2] [3] [4] [5]

3. The people who know me say I'm easy-going. I roll with things as they are. [1] [2] [3] [4] [5]

4. I find it tough to get the ball rolling on things, and rather than fight the status quo, I stay complacent. [1] [2] [3] [4] [5]

When you're done answering these questions, tally your scores for each type. Whichever type has the highest score is your dominant Enneagram type. Remember, you also have to consider your wings, so consider the next two high scores after your primary one. If the highest score is an 8, and your next highest score is a 7, that's a significant sign the second type is your wing.

## How to Avoid Mistyping

Mistyping happens when you think you're one Enneagram type, but you're another. This error is possible because you're working with a tool that considers your behaviors and the things that drive you to act how you do. Your behavior is something that can change. It can be affected by your culture, how you were brought up, what you have experienced so far, and how things are going for you.

You can mistype yourself when you find behaviors of a different type than yours relatable, but you're not connecting to the *why* that powers those behaviors. You may also mistype yourself when you feel more connected with your wings or the type you morph into when you're going through stress or growing into your best self.

Society and culture can cause mistyping, too. For instance, today's Western society values productivity, so you may identify with a type that is more productive than yours because you aspire to be like them and not because you are that type.

Gauging your correct type requires self-awareness. If you cannot dig within yourself and be honest, you may not get an accurate assessment when you use the questionnaire to determine your type. Also, speaking of questionnaires, they won't do any good without reflecting on your motivation in making the choices you do. So, how do you avoid mistyping?

1.  Become introspective. Take a long, hard look at your life so far. Consider the patterns that play out in your relationships and career. What is it

that drives you? What are you truly afraid of? What's the one thing you want the most in life? By taking the time to understand these things before taking a test or using a questionnaire, you're more likely to choose the correct type.

2. Continue to research the Enneagram. If you use only one book or blog, you may not have enough perspectives on how each type express-es itself, so you won't know if you're genuinely the type you think you are.

3. Pay close attention to why you do what you do. Your reasons matter more than what you do. Two people can save a cow for different reasons. One may want the cow to live, while the other wants fresh milk.

4. Speak with experts if you can. You can attend classes and workshops on the Enneagram to learn more and see if you've mistyped yourself. The experts will know what questions to ask you to determine your archetype.

5. Retake the test later. You may have life experi-ences demonstrating what type you are in the interim.

# Chapter 3:

## Applying the Enneagram in Daily Life

Everyone has something about them that remains consistent. It could be a pattern of thinking or acting. It could also be recurrent life themes. The Enneagram has a profound effect on your life when you work with it. This chapter will teach you how to use it for the best results.

## How the Enneagram Affects Your Life

**You Will Have Better Interactions with the People You Love.** When you understand your type, you'll know what causes you to interact with the people in your life the way you do. You are no longer driven by unconscious desires and fears because, thanks to the Enneagram, all those things come to light. If you're a Type 7, you understand your tendency to avoid pain at all costs and to chase after pleasure. Being conscious of this, you can choose a more empowered way to be with the people you care about.

**You'll Notice the Patterns That Govern Your Relationships, Too.** If you're a Type 3, you may be more interested in progressing in your career, to the detriment of your relationships, since you're the Achiever type. When you spot this tendency, you can check it and be more deliberate about reaching out to the people you love. If you're a Type 5, you'll understand why your response to getting chewed out or criticized is to pull away from everyone and do some investigation. In contrast, a Type 1 person would view the criticism as an opportunity to improve.

**You'll Become a Better Communicator.** Your communication style, whether non-confrontational or assertive, depends on your archetype. When you know how to communicate, you can see how to adjust. Handling conflicts becomes easier for you. If you're a Type 8, you may prefer to be direct and honest. However, a Type 9 would think you're coming off as aggressive. If you're communicating with a Type 6, you know, thanks to the Enneagram, that it would be best to reassure them and not be heavy-handed with the criticism. You become a more empathetic person.

**You'll Grow in Self-Awareness.** Since the Enneagram calls you to spot the tendencies you have, you can tell what you need to fix. You can also learn what traits you haven't taken advantage of to grow in your personal and spiritual life.

**Your Career Choices Will Be Better.** Since you know your type, you can tell which career choices would be best and which ones you should turn down. Are you an Investigator? You would be phenomenal in any career that requires you to do some research, and you'd have a great time because you love to be independent and learn a lot. The Enneagram will improve your interactions with your colleagues. When you use it to determine what to focus on in work, you'll experience job satisfaction beyond anything you've ever had.

**You Can Handle Stress Better with Your Enneagram.** What's stressful to one person is a breeze to another. Consider the Type 6 person. They don't do well when they sense danger, as it stresses them out. So, it would make sense for this person to craft a routine that helps them feel safe. Being stressed means you're following the path of disintegration. When you recognize this, you can use the best self-care processes for your type to move you back into integration. You'll know the best ways to release stress, whether seeking adventures if you're a 7 or spending quiet, alone time in nature if you're a 9.

## Real-Life Scenarios of the Enneagram's Impact on Relationships

**The Enneagram Can Assist You with Compatibility.** Consider Jake, who is an Enthusiast, and Eliza, who is a Helper. Naturally, Jake is up for new adventures anywhere, anytime. Eliza is a lover at heart, devoting her time to the people she holds dear. At first, Jake loved this about Eliza, and Eliza enjoyed her boyfriend's passion for spontaneous fun. However, Jake had trouble dealing with anything he felt was too difficult in terms of feelings, which meant Eliza had to do the emotional heavy lifting for both of them. She loves to be appreciated, but this desire leads to some squabbles. Eventually, by learning about their Enneagram types, they restored balance in their relationship. Jake learned to be more vocal in his appreciation for his partner, while Eliza made peace with Jake's desire for variety.

**Working with the Enneagram Can Help with Conflict Resolution.** It certainly did for Samantha and Owen. Samantha is a Challenger, while Owen is a Peacemaker. As a challenger, Sam's default is to be direct and honest. So, she has no problems with confrontation because she knows its value. However, Owen would rather have peace. If a storm is brewing, he turns his back on it and acts like it doesn't exist. When the two of them have a disagreement, Owen feels like Samantha is overbearing, so he goes into his shell, shutting her out. They wouldn't become aware of this issue until they learned about the Enneagram. Now, Owen knows Samantha's confrontations come from a place of love and a desire for clarity, and he's more willing to talk about his concerns instead of withdrawing. As for Sam, she understands she needs to take a softer approach when speaking with Owen about difficult issues.

## Practical Tips for Spiritual Growth

**Type 1:** You have a loud inner critic. It's time to ask it to keep quiet. If you find your inner critic pipes up again, remind yourself you're not it, and it's not always telling you the truth about who you are. Mindfulness meditation is an excellent way to start noticing when this voice pipes up in you and realize you aren't that voice. As you meditate, you learn not to give the critic your energy. Life is full of flaws and imperfections. You are part of life, so you're not exempt from being imperfect. It's okay not to have it all together. Moreover, learn to be more grateful. Decide that before you go to bed, you will find one thing about the day or your life that you appreciate. This way, you learn to stop giving so much attention to what's wrong. The more you focus on what's going well, the more things will work out.

**Type 2:** You are a gem in a world full of selfishness, but you must be mindful about giving so much you lose yourself. It's time to draw the line. Boundaries are your best friends, and upholding them is how you give back to yourself. Self-care practices will be a tremendous benefit to you. It's not selfish to take care of number one. Assume you're another person, and consider ways to treat yourself with kindness. You are worthy. You matter, regardless of whether you help others or not. Know that.

**Type 3:** You're quite the achiever, aren't you? As awesome as that is, you need some rest. All work and no play is a surefire way to get burned out. So, schedule some rest time. If it helps, think of rest as a form of work or a task. This way, you can bring the same passion to your rest that you do to work. You aren't defined by what you've accomplished. You're more than that. Decide to be authentic by letting people get to know who you are outside your achievements. Finally, try doing things for the fun of it and nothing else. Take part in activities with no goals and no need to be successful.

**Type 4:** Sometimes you get melancholic, lost in your intense emotions, desiring something ineffable that feels beyond your grasp. It's best to ground yourself, bring your awareness back to your body and the here and now. Take long, leisurely walks, or engage in activities where you work with your hands to stay in the moment. Whenever you get that familiar feeling of not-enoughness, you can use positive affirmations to remind yourself that you matter and are a unique soul. You should get a journal and make it a daily habit to write about your feelings. You'll notice your patterns and better handle the intense emotions you get.

**Type 5:** You love being in your head since investigating is your thing. However, you would benefit from stepping outside your mind now and then by working with your physical senses. Eat mindfully, tasting your food and feeling the textures. Go for a walk and notice how each step feels against the ground. Also, connect with others around you. Maybe you could attend a group meeting or workshop about one of your many interests. Finally, you should be firm with yourself by capping the time you spend learning about things. Instead, how about you put what you've already learned to work?

**Type 6:** You're a loyalist, so sometimes, you struggle with anxiety. You wonder about other people's motives, making your relationships less fulfilling than they could be. Take part in trust-building exercises. As for your fears, there's only one way to face them: Head on. Make a list of everything you're afraid of, from the least frightening to the most terrifying. Then, expose yourself to each item on the list, one after another, until you see you are a resilient person who can easily handle anything. You also have to be in the present. Sometimes, you catastrophize the future. By grounding yourself using deep breathing and other mindfulness techniques, you can keep a clear perspective and rid yourself of unnecessary concerns about the future.

**Type 7:** You're always stimulated, implying you don't fully immerse yourself in what's happening around you. So, whether you're eating, reading a book, or listening to something or someone, be deliberate about it. Bring all your attention to it. You won't get it right immediately, but with practice, you'll master the art of being present. Rather than spread yourself thin by seeking novelty and variety, skipping along the pond like a rock in whatever you're doing, how about you dive deep? You can choose a few things out of the many you're into and give them your all. Finally, you should learn to delay gratification in little things and big things, whether having your favorite meal or splurging on something you want. This way, you'll be more appreciative of those things when you get them.

**Type 8:** Your fire is beautiful, but sometimes it burns a little too hot, so people steer clear of your flames and don't get to know the real you. Be proactive about being vulnerable. Don't be afraid to show what you feel inside. If anything, you will attract the right people to you when you do this and banish the wrong ones so your relationships are established in truth. Before you let your impulses get the better of you, take a moment to think about how you're about to react. You could count to ten or take deep, calming breaths. Also, try active listening. Show other people you think their perspectives have value. It's much better than listening to see how you can take control or challenge the other person.

**Type 9:** You would be better off learning how to be assertive. You have needs, too, and like anyone else's, those needs deserve to be met. There are workshops you can attend to teach you assertiveness. It's a skill like any other, which means with practice, you can master it. Could you try moving more? Whether you're dancing to your favorite tune or sweating it out during a hot yoga session, movement is good for you. It will help you get in touch with what your body needs and what you desire in life. Finally, you can learn to make decisions. One way to do this is to allot time each day when you make clear decisions on things, whether small or big. By doing this, you'll be more confident in the choices you make.

# Chapter 4:

## The Enneagram as a Tool for Spiritual Development

The Enneagram can help you accomplish the spiritual growth and development you seek. Remember, once your spirit feels right, everything else falls into place. Your outer, physical world will morph into what you'd prefer when you handle your inner, spiritual world first. So, in this chapter, you'll learn how to use this system to develop your spiritual life.

**How the Enneagram Enriches Your Spiritual Life**

**The Enneagram Helps You Understand Your Unique Gifts and Obstacles.** These attributes are an intrinsic part of your soul. It's no accident you're designed the way you are. As you study yourself through the lens of your type, you'll recognize when you're acting from a place of authenticity versus when you're acting based on your ego's whims. If you're a Type 2, you may offer help to others only because you desire to be loved. However, your soul is the epitome of unconditional love. Your true self doesn't care whether that help is reciprocated or appreciated. When you give from your soul's perspective, you'll know the difference. You know you don't need anyone's validation or praise. You give because you love, and you love because you *are* love.

**You Can Become a More Compassionate Person.** The Enneagram does more than show you your life's trajectory. It shows you what you struggle with and what you long for. When you realize everyone has fears and desires, it's easier to view their actions and choices with a generous dose of compassion. Imagine having issues with a coworker who is a Type 5. You can't stand how aloof they are. However, when you learn they're an Investigator, which means they love their personal space and become worried and frustrated by others intruding on them, you'll see them with kinder eyes. You don't think of them as being full of themselves anymore. You realize they're doing all they can to keep themselves from feeling drained and empty.

**The Enneagram Can Teach You Empathy.** What's the difference between compassion and empathy? When you're empathetic toward someone, you go beyond understanding their plight to feeling it yourself. You step into their shoes and walk in them long enough to tell where their toes feel squished. Empathy goes deeper than compassion.

**You'll Discover the Connection between You and Everyone Else.** The Enneagram's diagram depicts the interconnectedness of all beings. You may have a primary type, but there are also wings, paths of integration and disintegration to consider. You flow through all of these, as you are a complex person who can't be neatly put in a box. The Enneagram shows a deep, spiritual truth: All of life is connected. Everyone influences everyone else. Today's world is one that seeks to keep people apart. You're never alone. You couldn't be, even if you tried.

**You Can Make Peace with Your Dark Side Using the Enneagram.** There's no such thing as a completely good person who's all love, light, rainbows, and glitter. When you come to the world as a child, it teaches you certain aspects of yourself are undesirable. As a child, you want to fit in. So you squash those aspects of yourself into a box and store it away. The thing is, you've still got the box. That box contains your shadow self. The shadow contains everything about yourself that you don't want to admit or face, as well as some gifts you've ignored because you were chastised for displaying or using them. As you work with the Enneagram, you come face to face with your shadow and bring it into the light by accepting it exists and is part of you.

**The Enneagram Shows You What You're to Focus on for Spiritual Growth.** Are you a Challenger? Your path to spiritual growth is clear. Allow yourself to be vulnerable. Are you an Achiever? Your goal is to learn to relax and breathe more and that you're worthy regardless of whether you're busy smashing goals or not. The Enneagram will show you the ugly garments you need to take off so your soul's light can shine through you.

## Spiritual Practices for Your Type

This section will show you the best spiritual practices for your type, so you can experience growth and see your life change for the better.

### Type 1: The Reformer

1. Basic meditation: Put all your attention on a candle's flame, a blank spot in the room, or your breath. This practice will feed your desire for discipline and developing focus. Do this daily.

2. Ritualistic prayer: You can do this however you like, as long as you practice it daily. You can

create a sequence of activities or prayer points and let that be a ritual. Prayer is great for helping you get clear on the right course of action.

3. Iyengar yoga: This form is about being precise in your movements and ensuring every part of your body lines up correctly in each move.

4. Judgment mindfulness: Begin noticing your judgments about things, ideas, and people. Yes, you are people, too. Your goal is to realize you have these judgments but choose not to act on them or make decisions influenced by them. This way, you'll become more compassionate to yourself and others.

## Type 2: The Helper

1. Loving Kindness Meditation: This form of meditation is also called Metta meditation. As you practice it, you'll become aware of how expansive love can be. Your love will extend beyond your circle to the world and yourself.

2. Self-love prayer: Pray each day. Your prayers should center around loving yourself. Pray to your higher self or whatever power you believe in to deepen your love for yourself. With time, you'll take care of yourself like you help others.

3. Karma yoga: This form is about doing things for others with no expectations.

4. Needs mindfulness: Notice your needs when they come up. Notice your typical inclination to ignore them. Sit with the feeling that wells up in you as you identify this need and the habit that makes you deny yourself. Then, choose to honor that need somehow, no matter how little.

## Type 3: The Achiever

1. Mantra meditation: Write affirmations in your words that state you are not your achievements but are far more than them. Repeat these daily.

2. Humility prayer: Your prayers should revolve around becoming more humble. When you're humble, you stop the lifelong show you've been putting on for everyone and become your authentic self.

3. Power yoga: This form of yoga is dynamic, requiring strength for each move, and you'll enjoy it because of how goal-oriented you are.

4. Motives mindfulness: Before you take action, become aware of why. What drives the action?

If it's coming from a place of performance, you can let it go. If it's from an authentic place, do it.

## Type 4: The Individualist

1. Contemplative meditation: This form of meditation requires sitting with your innermost feelings. Observe them. Notice where they come from. Consider the first time you remember feeling each emotion in your life, and see if you can find a different perspective on whatever led you to feel that way.

2. Emotional prayer: The only structure to this prayer is to do it daily. Allow yourself to have honest conversations with your higher self. Don't sugarcoat anything while you pray. Be emotionally honest.

3. Bhakti yoga: Practicing this type of yoga will deepen your emotional connection with your higher power. It's an excellent way to channel those deep emotions you feel.

4. Grounding mindfulness: Any practice that will root you in the present is good. Move your body, walk in nature, and notice the crunch of the leaves beneath your feet. Practice body

awareness by bringing your attention to each body part, from your feet to your head.

## Type 5: The Investigator

1.  Transcendental meditation: This form of meditation helps you go beyond your normal patterns of thoughts and experience what it's like to just *be.* You become pure consciousness or awareness, with no judgments or thoughts. This meditation will help you find the off button and rest your mind.

2.  Reflective prayer: Daily, pray to the divine or your higher self to help you be more understanding. You may also read spiritual writings and reflect on what you've learned.

3.  Jnana yoga: This yoga is excellent for you and your cerebral tendencies. It's about getting knowledge and contemplating it to mine the gems of wisdom contained within.

4.  Sensory mindfulness: Use your senses mindfully. Look around you for certain colors or shapes. What can you smell? How does your skin feel? How does your body feel in general? What can you taste when you eat? What are the textures

like? What sounds can you hear? Which ones are easy to pick up, and which are more subtle?

## Type 6: The Loyalist

1. Guided meditation: This meditation will help you feel secure. You'll appreciate having someone walk you through it. Many free guided meditations are available online, but you can also work with an experienced guide in person.

2. Security prayer: Each day, say prayers that affirm you are safe. These prayers should help you learn that true security comes from within. Pray for the ability and courage to be more trusting.

3. Hatha yoga: With this yoga form, there's a balance between how you breathe and the postures you hold. You'll enjoy this thoroughly because it will ground you and help you let go of your anxious thoughts.

4. Grounding mindfulness: Do any exercise that roots you in the present moment. Anything that takes you out of your head and forces you to notice your body and be present is great.

## Type 7: The Enthusiast

1. Movement meditations: You can meditate while you move your body. You may walk, dance, sway, or move however you'd like while being present.

2. Celebratory prayers: Your daily prayers should be thankful and joyful. As you pray, acknowledge the wonderful things in your life and feel the gratitude flooding your body.

3. Vinyasa flow yoga: This form of yoga involves moving from pose to pose in a fluid way. It's dynamic and perfect for the Enthusiast.

4. Savoring mindfulness: The goal is to plunge yourself deeply into the beautiful, awesome experiences in your life so you can enjoy them. If nothing is happening now, you can do this with past experiences. If you're enjoying something in the moment, like a meal, savor it by noticing the obvious and subtle flavors and textures.

## Type 8: The Challenger

1. Body scan meditation: For this meditation, scan your body with your mind, beginning from your feet and working your way up. Notice any

tension? Tense the muscles there, and as you exhale, allow them to loosen. Keep going until you get to the crown of your head.

2. Wisdom prayers: Ask your higher self to give you the wisdom you need to lead people in a way that benefits everyone. Pray for the strength to champion others' causes and uplift them.

3. Ashtanga yoga: You love a challenge, so why not have a practice that pushes you? This yoga requires discipline and will push you to be better.

4. Vulnerability mindfulness: Each day, look for opportunities to be vulnerable. Since you enjoy challenges, make a game of it. Each time you share something, notice how you feel more at home with being vulnerable than before.

## Type 9: The Peacemaker

1. Choiceless awareness meditation: Sit and allow your mind to do its thing. Unlike other forms of meditation, you're not focusing on anything. All you're doing is observing all the random thoughts without examining or getting attached to any of them.

2.  Clarity and courage prayer: Always pray daily to have clarity in your life and the courage to speak up for yourself when you need something.

3.  Yin yoga: This yoga is slow. It puts you in a meditative state and allows you to introspect. You hold passive poses for extended periods, allowing you to connect to your inner world and learn what needs you've suppressed.

4.  Decision mindfulness: Actively make decisions for yourself. The more you do this, the more you'll realize there is no right or wrong path. There's only the path that calls to you the most, and even if it doesn't turn out as you expected, it's not a big deal. That's life.

Whatever type you are, you will benefit tremendously from growing spiritually and personally. While everything originates from the spirit world, you should also work on growing as a person. This holistic approach to self-realization will give you results beyond your wildest expectations.

# Chapter 5:

## Overcoming Challenges and Embracing Transformation

Discovering the truth about yourself is a necessary step toward changing for the better. However, this is no mean feat. You'll need loads of courage as you mind the depths of your Enneagram type for the truth about yourself. In the process, you'll come up against an opponent tougher and more powerful than any other you could have in life: Your mind. Specifically, it's the inner voice in your head that tells you you're not good enough. It points out all the evidence it can find around you to prove its point about your unworthiness. It whispers in your ears, telling you your dreams are too big, you're being ridiculous, and going down the path of self-realization will only lead to the worst outcomes. It gets pretty lippy for something that talks without an actual mouth. Your job is to shut it up and then shut it down. As you use the Enneagram, it will reflect the good *and* the bad about yourself. It will show you your superpowers and your kryptonite. It's not easy staring the naked truth about yourself in the face.

However, you should embark on this journey with the right perspective. It will suck at times, but embrace that. Think of it like working out. In the heat of the moment, you're breaking down your muscles, breathing hard. Ultimately, your muscles rebuild themselves, bigger and stronger than ever. Your lung capacity improves, and you can handle whatever comes your way. With your Enneagram, you'll do the most challenging workout yet: Facing your shadows. However, when you come out on the other side, you will be more powerful, stronger, and resilient. If you want to make it out on the other side, you need to be ready for the doubts, fears, and obstacles that come your way. Don't back down. Keep your eyes on the prize, and understand that challenges change you for the better.

## Common Challenges to Contend With

**You May Fight the Change to Come.** Most people say they'd like to change something, yet resist the change they seek. This tendency is human nature. Expect resistance, and you'll be ready to nip it in the bud. Resistance is fueled by a desire to remain in your comfort zone rather than venture outside to see the goodness waiting for you. What's so wrong with wanting to be comfortable? Isn't that why anyone does anything? Well, if you dig past the tinsel of promised comfort, you'll notice the truth is you have a fear of the unknown.

You can interpret the energy that comes with fear as excitement with a shift in perspective. So, con your mind into assuming it's actually excited for the changes to come, not afraid of them. You can use affirmations to help you with this process. The affirmations work best when you're not gripped by fear or anxiety, so do them when you're feeling good, and you'll handle the fearful times like a pro. Also, remember that whenever you resist the change you seek, you accept a mediocre existence. No one was born to be mediocre. You deserve to be the best version of yourself you can envision and more. So, flip the fear and resistance on their heads and let them drive you to plunge deeper into the ocean of your Enneagram type.

**You May Be Afraid of Being Vulnerable.** Make this your new mantra: There is strength in vulnerability. It's more courageous to let your guard down than to mount walls to shut everyone out. If you think about it, you're keeping yourself locked in, which is an admission of weakness. So, since strength is a virtue you admire and aspire to have, open up. Allow yourself to face the demons you fear, and you may surprise yourself by defeating them and learning you're stronger than you think. Vulnerability will help you grow, not ruin you. It's a powerful force, and it will catapult you to undeniable heights when you lean into it.

**You May Struggle with Your Old Habits.** These habits are like well-worn grooves in your brain. Your neurons are used to traveling the same old paths. It's easy and comfortable. However, you must change your habits if you want new results. As the saying goes, "Insanity is doing the same thing over and over again and expecting different results." These habits have to be broken and replaced with new ones. It's not going to be an easy process. There will be days you want to quit and go back to being your old self. Sometimes, you'll give in to that inner siren song calling you back to your old ways and the comfort of the good old days. Recognize the lyrics to that song are only sweet nothings. There's nothing for you back there. The only way to go is forward and upward. Shut that voice down as if your life depends on it because it really does. If you don't like where you are right now, it's time to do things differently. It's time to be different.

# How to Overcome these Challenges

1. **Be Accountable to Yourself.** Get a journal for your Enneagram journey. Start the day writing the goals you want to accomplish. At night, write about your progress. Be honest with yourself, even if the truth isn't pretty. Your honesty should be rooted in self-compassion, not self-loathing. This way, you have no hesitation in calling things as you see them and making the necessary changes along the way.

2. **Get Comfy with the Discomfort.** Make a point of doing something each day that gives you that squirmish, uncomfortable feeling in the pit of your stomach or that scares you. It could be drinking some bitters, taking a cold shower, or practicing intermittent fasting (with medical permission and supervision, of course). You could choose a hard workout. As you do these things, you show yourself you're a resilient person who can handle anything, including the discomfort of personal and spiritual growth.

3. **Use the 40 Percent Rule.** Some days, you'll feel you've peaked and can't go any further with your journey. Remember, you're only ever using

40 percent of your abilities. In other words, you can push past the wall you hit. If you like, make a game of proving your mind wrong each day. When you hit a wall, get excited. It means you're about to uncover new levels of mental strength and resilience you never knew you had.

4. **Envision Your Ideal Self.** When you start this journey, take a moment to consider what the best version of yourself is like. How does this version dress? How do they speak? How do they feel about others, and what are their interactions like? When you have this vision clear in your mind, you guarantee yourself success.

5. **Draw Strength from Your Memories.** Think about the tough things you've contended with in life and how you overcame them. If the going gets tough and rough, reach into your memory bank and remind yourself you've handled worse. If you got through those past challenges, you can and will get through this one, too.

6. **Use Mantras.** Rather than choose something generic, create one you resonate with. You can affirm that you are becoming your true self more and more every day. Use these mantras

daily, and with time, they'll become your automatic way of thinking.

7. **Take It Bit by Bit.** You have to figure out your type, then your wings, and finally, your integration and disintegration paths. There's a lot to handle. So, break it down and take your time with the process.

8. **Learn Everything You Can About the Enneagram.** Make it a point to devour all the information you can. Join forums and workshops on the subject so you can learn from different perspectives and pick valuable information that could help you.

9. **Reflect on Your Life Through the Enneagram Each Day.** You only need a few minutes to accomplish this. Think about your choices, actions, and responses, viewing them through the lens of your type. You'll learn interesting things about yourself.

10. **Find Others on the Same Journey of Self-Discovery.** It's lovely to have people you can share your experiences with. Moreover, you'll have valuable insights for one another that no one may have discovered on their own. Finally, it's

nice to know other people are experiencing and working through the same challenges you are.

## Set Meaningful Intentions

You came to this world to live, not merely exist or act as an extra in someone else's movie. You're here to leave a mark. The way to accomplish that goal is to set intentions. How do you do this?

**Begin with Your Why**. Why do you desire to be a better person? Why does it matter to you to change who you are? Your why will be your North Star if you feel lost along your journey. When you are confused about what you're doing, your why will be there, cutting through the fog with its radiant light, beckoning you toward the end goal. Whatever you want to accomplish in life, do as Simon says, and *start with why.*

**Mold Your Legacy.** When you have your why figured out, consider the end goal. What sort of mark would you like to leave on the world? Fast forward to your last moments. What would matter the most to you? How would you like to be remembered, not only by those near and dear to you but by everyone else on this little blue dot? In other words, what will your legacy be?

**Fall in Love with Hard.** Unlike other books, this one won't lie to you to make you feel good. Change isn't easy. Growth isn't either, nor is it linear. Sometimes, you'll want to take that legacy you hope to create, rip it to shreds, and forget this "Enneagram nonsense." Don't be fooled into thinking you're the one with those impulses. That's your old self. It's your ego fighting for its life because it is terrified. It knows it will be replaced at the end of this journey. Don't let it scare you away from the process. Accept that it will be gritty, and plunge yourself into it anyway.

**Make Each Day Count.** There are no off days on the journey of personal and spiritual growth. You should do at least one thing each day that helps you become better. Even if all you can manage is to read a page of a good book, listen to five minutes of a podcast, or help one person. Each day, deliberately take one step forward.

**Keep Going.** At some point, you'll achieve your intention. That's not the end, though. You should set another intention for yourself. If you don't, you'll become complacent, and one day, you won't be able to explain how you found yourself right back where you started. There's always a new way to grow. There's always more you can be, so enjoy the never-ending process of expansion.

**Share.** As you embark on this journey, you'll experience highs and lows, ups and downs, and everything in between. Your experiences can inspire others to grow. They can help people see their potential. People are waiting for you to shine your light so they can see the path to their self-actualization, too. They can only do that if you share your experiences authentically and honestly. Don't airbrush or sugarcoat them. Don't try to make it seem all good. Remember, you don't put on a show anymore. You are unapologetically real.

# Conclusion

You've come to the end of this book, but this is the start of a profound change in your life. As you begin your transformation, remember the Enneagram is more than a tool. Use this as a companion to help you in every aspect of your life. You can and should learn more about the Enneagram so your journey is more rewarding. As you work with this tool, you'll get interesting revelations about yourself. Some insights that come to you as you work with this system will jolt you, making you feel as if you've been sleeping your way through life the entire time you've been here. Even when you think you're awake, you'll find you can be *more* awake as time passes. You'll discover truths that force you to question how you've always seen life.

The Enneagram will do all this for you and more, helping you evolve. It's not something you use once and get rid of. You'll need this as a companion for the rest of your life to grow in self-understanding each day. Remember, your journey never ends. The depths of truth you discover with the Enneagram are deeper than you can imagine. As you apply these truths to your life, you'll always find higher heights to attain. This tool will shine a light on all that is dark and hidden in your psyche so you can use your discoveries about yourself to become the person you have always wished you could be.

**A Final Note:** Do not allow the Enneagram type you think you are to define you. It's a tool you can use to understand your authentic self. You will change and evolve throughout your life, so you shouldn't be so adamant about fitting yourself into one of the types. When your circumstances change, repeat the Enneagram test and see what's new. With that said, enjoy the journey to the best version of yourself yet.

# References

Chestnut, B. (2013). The complete Enneagram: 27 paths to greater self-knowledge. She Writes Press.

Daniels, D., & Price, V. (2009). The essential Enneagram: The definitive personality test and self-discovery guide. HarperOne.

Heuertz, C. (2017). The sacred Enneagram: Finding your unique path to spiritual growth. Zondervan.

Hurley, K., & Dobson, T. (1991). What's my type?. HarperOne.

Maitri, S. (2000). The spiritual dimension of the Enneagram: Nine faces of the soul. TarcherPerigee

Palmer, H. (1991). The Enneagram: Understanding yourself and the others in your life. HarperCollins

Palmer, H. (1995). The Enneagram in love and work: Understanding your intimate and business relationships. HarperOne.

Riso, D. R., & Hudson, R. (1996). Personality types: Using the Enneagram for self-discovery. Houghton Mifflin Harcourt

Riso, D. R., & Hudson, R. (2003). Discovering your personality type: The essential introduction to the Enneagram. Houghton Mifflin Harcourt